INDUSTRIAL RELATIONS IN CONDITIONS OF FULL EMPLOYMENT

INDUSTRIAL RELATIONS IN CONDITIONS OF FULL EMPLOYMENT

by

H. S. KIRKALDY

MONTAGUE BURTON PROFESSOR OF
INDUSTRIAL RELATIONS

AN INAUGURAL LECTURE
DELIVERED AT CAMBRIDGE ON
16 OCTOBER 1945

CAMBRIDGE
AT THE UNIVERSITY PRESS
1945

CAMBRIDGE
UNIVERSITY PRESS

University Printing House, Cambridge CB2 8BS, United Kingdom

Published in the United States of America by Cambridge University Press, New York

Cambridge University Press is part of the University of Cambridge.

It furthers the University's mission by disseminating knowledge in the pursuit of
education, learning and research at the highest international levels of excellence.

www.cambridge.org
Information on this title: www.cambridge.org/9781107676268

© Cambridge University Press 1945

First published 1945
Re-issued 2014

A catalogue record for this publication is available from the British Library

ISBN 978-1-107-67626-8 Paperback

INDUSTRIAL RELATIONS
IN CONDITIONS
OF FULL EMPLOYMENT

MANY of those whose duty and honour it is to deliver an Inaugural Lecture from a professorial chair in this University
are able to survey in retrospect the contribution to the same
field of learning of a long line of predecessors famous in
their day and time or in the estimate of history. In so doing
they are able to pay honour where honour is due, to trace in
broad outline the development of their subject, to draw
sometimes a striking contrast between different points in
history and to provide a point of departure for their own
studies and teaching. The problems of industrial relations
are as old as industry itself and have been the subject of
study, particularly on the abstract and theoretical side, by
many eminent economists, but the systematic study in this
and other universities of the practical problems involved in
the relations between employers and employed, the causes
of industrial disputes and the methods of promoting industrial peace is of comparatively recent date. In entering
on the duties of the Montague Burton Chair of Industrial
Relations I must seek my inspiration from a single previous
occupant and to him must my tribute be paid. I too would
draw a contrast but, if like is to be compared with like, it
cannot be derived from conditions in past centuries.
Changes in the scale of organisation of the parties to industrial relations have been of such magnitude, changes in

methods have been of so fundamental a nature, as to require within the memory of most of us an entirely new approach to the problems of industrial relations and to leave us without any sure foundation in the lessons of the past.

I take courage, however, in the example of one whose modesty impelled him in his Inaugural Lecture before this University to say:

'And now, Sir, the terrible moment is come when your ξένος must render some account—I will not say of himself, for that cannot be attempted—but of his business here. Well, first let me plead that while you have been infinitely kind to the stranger, feasting him and casting a gown over him, one thing not all your kindness has been able to do. With precedents, with traditions such as other Professors enjoy, you could not furnish him. The Chair is a new one, or almost new, and for the present would seem to float in the void, like Mahomet's coffin....For me, then, if you put questions concerning the work of this Chair, I must take example from the artist in *Don Quixote*, who being asked what he was painting answered modestly, "That is as it may turn out".'

These were the words of Sir Arthur Quiller-Couch and, if I have strayed so early from my own field, I find comfort in returning to it with the knowledge that the Chair of Industrial Relations in the University of Cambridge, though it dates only from 1931, had as its first occupant one who in his character set the example on which real success in industrial relations can alone be founded. The millions who heard in their homes the voice of John Hilton, though they may have known little of his diffidence in what we choose to call real life, may have glimpsed something of the qualities of his greatness. The essential factor in the life of John

Hilton was his humanity. The secret of his success in handling the problems of industrial relations was his understanding of the working people. He remembered that his subject-matter concerned not a commodity but his fellow men.

My purpose, however, in referring to my predecessor is not merely to pay a tribute to his qualities but to draw a contrast between the industrial circumstances in which he delivered his Inaugural Lecture and those in which I deliver mine. It is only fourteen years since he delivered the lecture which was the inauguration both of this Chair and of his tenure of it. He spoke at a time when the number of unemployed persons in this country had reached $2\frac{3}{4}$ millions and was to rise still higher; his subject was unemployment. I speak at a time when unemployment in this country has practically ceased to exist and I choose as my subject the problems of industrial relations in conditions of full employment.

The circumstances in which we have at the moment achieved a condition of full employment are of course those of a war economy still persisting into the first few months of peace; the circumstances in which we shall no doubt retain it for some years to come are those, firstly, of reconversion and, secondly, of reconstruction during which the devastation of war has to be repaired and vast arrears of capital equipment and maintenance have to be overtaken. When we speak of full employment, however, we contemplate the conditions neither of war nor of its immediate aftermath and turn our thoughts to a later stage when full employment can be accompanied by a rising standard of living. Full employment can be achieved in time of war; full employment accompanied by a rising standard of living can be achieved only in time of peace.

It does not fall within the scope of this Chair, as I understand it, to treat of the financial, technical and international measures necessary for the achievement and maintenance of full employment. These measures will, however, not succeed unless they are accompanied by harmonious relations. The peace required for the realisation of a rising standard of living in conditions of full employment is not merely peace between nations. There must also be peace within industry.

Attention and determination are concentrated on the goal of full employment in a way they have never been in the past. Nationally and internationally the achievement of full employment has now been declared to be a major preoccupation of governments—second only to, and a necessary condition of, the maintenance of international peace. The world looks forward to an era when the technical conditions necessary for the avoidance of unemployment in the midst of unsatisfied needs will be achieved. The worker in the field of industrial relations is called upon to prepare for the problems which will face him in conditions of full employment.

In the past, industrial relations have been in essence a trial of strength between opposing forces. What is the likely strength of these forces in the years which lie ahead? Statistics of membership of employers' associations are not available, but it is known that their position has been strengthened during the war. The latest figures show a membership of trade unions of over 8 millions and, although this does not equal the peak figure reached in 1920, it compares with a membership of under 5 millions ten years ago. Full employment should enable a membership figure of the order of 8 millions to be maintained and possibly even increased. On the other hand, as has been pointed out by Mr Lipson, the rapid growth of trade unions in the latter part of the eighteenth century was associated with the relaxation of state control over economic life and it will be interesting to see whether, in a planned economy, trade unionism will continue to flourish as vigorously as hitherto. Wide extension of compulsory social insurance under the aegis of the State may also lessen the emphasis which the trade union movement has in the past placed on its mutual insurance and friendly benefit activities and so weaken an important stabilising influence in trade union membership. The strength of the opposing forces will however clearly be greater than it was before the war. The establishment of bodies such as the various Catering Wages Boards and the enactment of the Wages Councils Act make it evident that the field in which unregulated wages will operate will be exceedingly small and that in future wages will in general be regulated either by collective bargaining or by decision of statutory boards.

Strength of opposing forces need not necessarily lead to open conflict. It may indeed act as a deterrent, more especially if it is known that the ranks of both armies are well-disciplined. Respect for the power of an opponent is often the precursor of an alliance. The existing basis of organisation of employers and workers in autonomous associations by separate industries and trades does not favour a general alliance. Sectional alliances of employers and employed in individual industries, if they emerge, must not be allowed to develop into wars of exploitation against other industries and the community. If a higher standard of living is to be achieved for those engaged in all industries and not merely for some—or indeed for none—internecine strife and wars of exploitation must equally be avoided.

Whatever may result from the development in the industrial sphere, as in the community as a whole, of a more humane and enlightened attitude or, to be more cynical, from respect for the enhanced strength of an opponent, it is clear that full employment will not of itself render industrial relations more harmonious. Professor Hilton was able in his Inaugural Lecture to point out that there was at that time peace in industry and to state that the relations of employers and employed were not then causing anxiety. It was, as he said, an uneasy peace but it was peace of a kind.

When discussing the problems of full employment it is necessary to postulate certain assumptions as to the framework within which society will operate. In particular it is necessary to assume that full employment is not to be attained by the sacrifice of the essential liberties of the worker or of the citizen, and it may also be assumed that it is the intention of the State to carry through an important programme of extension of social insurance and various forms of State subvention to the family in cash and in kind.

The first of these assumptions is clearly in keeping with the spirit of the people, and writers on full employment accept it as a necessary limitation on planning. One may perhaps discern a tendency among them to discard as unessential all liberties of which their particular plan would require the surrender and it would be wise not to assume too readily the willingness of the people to be deprived of accustomed liberties even as the price for full employment. Full employment in a slave state is comparatively easy of achievement. The problems of industrial relations in such a state would be capable of settlement in a summary fashion. It may be vexing to the planner that man is not prepared at times to work at the trade, in the place and under the conditions which it is clearly demonstrable would be in the best material interests of himself and of society, but it is well to realise that the ultimate judge on this earth of the essential liberties of man is man himself and not the planner.

The importance of the second assumption—an extended system of social security—lies in the fact that social security is at the same time an important element in the concept of a rising standard of living and an obstacle in the way of securing it. A rising standard of living assumes increasing production, and increasing production will depend largely on increased incentive to produce. Social security is in itself a part of this rising standard of living, and the opportunity to secure it by increased production would provide the incentive if incentive could operate on the community as a whole. The measure of success of incentives to production has however depended in the past, if we leave out of account times of great emotional and patriotic crisis, on the proximity of the direct benefit the individual worker or the small group of workers secures from the increased effort which he or the group exerts. Such proximity does not exist in relation to social security benefits. Greater effort on the part of an individual worker does not increase his social security benefits in any significant degree. On the contrary, the taxation necessary to finance such schemes has a very evident effect on his earnings and particularly on the portion of his earnings attributable to any greater effort he exerts. Social security, like full employment itself, provides therefore one more problem for those charged with the conduct of industrial relations. It is their task not only to secure industrial peace if our real objectives are to be attained, but also so to arrange matters that there is adequate incentive to increasing production. Concern with the problem of distributing the National Income should not be allowed to obscure the even more vital problem of increasing the National Income.

The idealist may hope that satisfaction with the structure and control of industry may in the future provide a sufficient incentive for the great majority. The realist while not less hopeful will, I think, address himself to more material considerations lest such hopes be falsified.

There is no need to seek far to discover the reasons why full employment will bring difficult problems for industrial relations, but the point may best be illustrated by a survey of the main causes of industrial disputes resulting in stoppages of work. The three main groups of such causes are, first, failure to agree on wages questions; second, union, inter-union and demarcation questions; and, third, what for want of a better name may be described as disciplinary questions. These three groups of causes were responsible in 1938 and 1939 for approximately 95 % of the stoppages recorded by the Ministry of Labour. The desire of the workers and of their unions in a period of depression to maintain and improve their position on such matters is certainly not less than in a period of prosperity, but their strength and ability to do so is reduced; the fear of unemployment diminishes the length to which a worker will go to enforce even what he believes to be his rights; unemployment provides an iron rod of discipline. Throughout the period of high unemployment which characterised the inter-war years it was rarely, apart from such an occasion as the General Strike of 1926, that the number of working days lost by industrial disputes reached serious magnitude. In only one year from 1927 onwards did the number of working days lost, as recorded by the Ministry of Labour, exceed 7 millions and in eight of the thirteen years from 1927 to 1939 the number was under 2 millions.

The object of drawing attention to these facts is not to advocate unemployment in order that the task may be made easy of those who are charged with the responsibility of conducting industrial negotiations, but to emphasise the urgency of the task which lies to the hand of employers, workers and the State in ensuring that the methods and machinery of industrial relations are perfected, that no needless sources of friction impede their operation, and that there is full realisation of the magnitude of the responsibility vesting in all parties to industrial negotiations.

Let us first turn to wages, which provide the greatest source of disputes leading to open conflict in industrial relations and at the same time the principal field for incentives to greater production. Full employment in any sense in which there is competition between unsatisfied demands for labour will undoubtedly present serious inflationary possibilities on the one hand or serious possibilities of industrial conflict on the other. The limits for increased remuneration which is not based on increased production are narrow. The spectacle of the employer resisting claims in circumstances when his whole need is for additional labour is unlikely to be seen. Moreover, the spectacle of an industry resisting wages demands which it as an industry can meet by passing on the cost to the consumer, refusing increases on lofty grounds of public interest and preaching elementary economic principles is a peculiarly irritating one to the worker and to the trade union official.

There were occasions during the war when industries producing for the Government account resisted wages demands which they might have met without difficulty by charging the Government more for the munitions of war or by reducing the Treasury receipts of Excess Profits. Resistance to such claims, even in cases where it was based on genuine belief that compliance was contrary to the national interest, did untold harm to industrial relations in the industries concerned. It placed upon employers a responsibility that was not rightfully theirs. There are limits to the extent that the individual employer or even the employers' association in a single industry should be regarded as trustee for the community. The strain of performing such a service unaided in conditions of full employment may well prove too great for the present machinery of industrial relations. If there is to be trusteeship, it must be joint trusteeship and it must be on a wider basis than that of the individual industry.

The urgent problem of industrial relations in the sphere of wages in conditions of full employment is to relieve the immediate parties of some measure of responsibility in regard to claims which raise important issues of national finance. In short, there is need for a *national* wages policy. The need was evident in conditions of full employment in war time; it will become more evident in conditions of full employment in peace. In war time some limits were set to competition for labour and therefore to wages by the effective control which the State exercised over the movement of labour; inflationary possibilities were held in check by rationing and price control.

A number of industries relate their wages to the Cost of Living Index or some other automatic factor, and to that extent there exists a wages policy, whether it is a right policy or not. Even in these cases however, the automatic factor is rarely the sole, or even the most important, means of wages adjustment. For the bulk of industries there is no wages policy within the industry itself nor is there for the nation as a whole. The mechanism of readjustment of the general level of wages merely is that a wages claim is tabled in one or more of the larger industries; it is debated at length on factors some relevant but mostly irrelevant; a frequent argument is comparison with other industries; it is ultimately decided on an assessment by the opposing side of the minimum concession which will avert industrial conflict. Thereafter lesser industries, with more or less friction, follow suit until the relative position in the bulk of industries is restored. Then follows a period of tranquillity of varying duration until the workers who tabled the original claim point out that their position in comparison with other industries is now no better than when their previous claim was discussed; and thereupon the process recommences. It operates, *mutatis mutandis*, in relation to claims for wages decreases.

In the course of all this, factors relevant to the particular industry, such as its ability to pay and the relativity of different grades, have their influence on the ultimate settlement, but there is no conscious *national* policy other than that of emulation. Such methods may have been sufficient for the minor and at times almost imperceptible adjustments by which the wage structure was determined prior to the war of 1914—1918; they may have been sufficient during the high unemployment which marked the inter-war years; they appear likely to be wholly inadequate to meet the conditions of full employment. It was the hope of many that a national wages policy might result from the decisions during the war of the National Arbitration Tribunal. The inability of the industrial negotiator to discern any such policy may arise from the fact that it has been the practice of the Tribunal not to give a reasoned judgment on the cases which have come before it. Possibly, however, it may be the case that these decisions have not been intended to enunciate any national wages policy but have been based merely on the expediency of the moment and the paramount necessity of avoiding in the midst of a war any stoppages in the munition industries. The National Arbitration Tribunal, even if it had desired to enunciate a national wages policy, would in any event have been powerless to make it effective. No national wages policy and no national wages authority can be effective in this country when there is excluded from its scope, as there was in practice if not in theory from that of the National Arbitration Tribunal, the coal mining industry. The powers of the National Arbitration Tribunal were greatly limited too by the fact that its consent was not necessary for a wages adjustment, whatever its magnitude, upon which the employers and workers in the industry concerned were in agreement and whatever might be the consequences in other industries of such an adjustment.

The difficulties of effective wages control in a democratic country are however even more clearly demonstrated by the wartime experience of the United States of America. In the United States, subject to certain specified exceptions, the consent of the National War Labor Board was required for wages adjustments even if the employer and worker were in agreement to make them. As a result also of Executive Orders and of decisions of the National War Labor Board, certain criteria were established which constituted for the United States a national wages policy in war time and which were described as a ceiling on wages. While the ceiling held reasonably fast, internal pressure tended at times to demonstrate that there are other and more normal exits than through the roof.

It is not on these lines that a national wages policy in a democratic country could work in times of peace with any real hope of success. Such a policy involves compulsory arbitration on disputes and even where no dispute exists. It involves in the last resort State regulation of wages in all trades and occupations. Compulsory arbitration or State regulation involves as a logical consequence compulsory enforcement of decisions and prohibition of strikes and lock-outs. Decisions are not in fact enforceable against a body of workers which is strenuously opposed to their terms. Voluntary arbitration has its place in industrial relations as has also State regulation for imposing minimum conditions in unorganised trades, but compulsion will not be an acceptable system for workers who have been accustomed themselves individually or collectively to say whether they approve the terms on which it is proposed they should work.

Any attempt to evolve a national wages policy, if it is to have hope of success, should take the form of guidance rather than compulsion. The policy itself should if possible be laid down in agreement between the central national organisations of the employers and workers, the British Employers' Confederation and the Trades Union Congress. If that is not possible, it should be worked out by independent persons of established reputation in finance, economics and industry who have the confidence of employers and workers. It is not for me to say what such a national wages policy should be or the factors on which it should be based, but it would not be advisable that it should attempt to do more than recommend to industry from time to time in broad outline the nature of the wages policy to be pursued and state the reasons on which the recommendations are based. Recommendations of this nature could play an important part in limiting the field of controversy within industry and in evolving a conscious wages policy to replace the haphazard methods which exist to-day.

The tasks of handling industrial relations successfully in conditions of full employment and of securing the increased production necessary for a rising standard of living call also in many industries for a radical revision and simplification of the wage structure, for extended use of systems of payment by results and for greater uniformity between the different industries with regard to overtime rates. Simplification of the wage structure and extension of payment by results may seem mutually exclusive, but they must be reconciled if maximum production is to be obtained and disharmony avoided. Much of the complication of wages systems arises from historical sources; expedients necessary at a time when revision of the wage system is not possible are perpetuated; additions to wages which it is hoped may be only temporary are kept apart from base rates long after it is clear that they have become permanent additions to wages; forms of wages which were incentives at the time of their introduction are retained long after their incentive power has disappeared.

Systems of payment by results, while a normal incident of some industries, are a source of acute controversy in others. If instituted and operated on a basis of willing co-operation they can provide an important incentive to greater utilisation of costly capital equipment and to greater output. One of the difficulties of systems of payment by results in industries where there are not standard products or standard methods of production is the necessity of fixing piece work rates at the individual works. This leads often before long to remarkable divergences in the earnings at different works in the same industry of workers performing work of equal value and skill. It means, moreover, that control over the negotiation of rates ceases to be a function of the central organisations of the employers and workers in the industry. If the difficulties of increasing the range of nationally negotiated piece work rates can be overcome, there will at the same time be overcome much of the

hostility which systems of payment by results have en-
countered and many of the anomalies they have pro-
duced.

Overtime and week-end work have in recent years become
a frequent source of dispute. The embargo on overtime has
become a common alternative to the strike as a means of
enforcing wages claims quite unconnected with overtime
itself. In times of full employment and shortage of labour
not only will the need for overtime be more pressing in order
to cope with fluctuating demand but the willingness to work
it will be reduced. A clear distinction must be drawn
between so-called overtime which is merely working the
normal weekly hours, but on a rota including night work or
week-end work, and overtime constituting an extension of
normal working hours. Subject to such considerations,
there is no valid reason for existing disparities between the
inducement offered in different industries and even within
the same industry for overtime work. Their removal, like
many other unjustifiable inequalities in working conditions,
would help to limit the field of controversy in industrial
relations.

In relation to wages one of the greatest factors limiting
incentive is the present level and method of taxation. The
matter is one between the worker and the State, but the
odium which attaches to the tax collector has played its
part in rendering relations more difficult between the worker
and the employer who now acts as the unpaid agent of the
State in collection of Income Tax. The remedies, like those
of many other disturbing factors in industrial relations, are
outside the scope of industrial relations themselves. The
obvious solution is reduced taxation, but there is also need
for reform of a system which applies a highest and penal
rate of taxation to that part of income attributable to the

hours which it is most difficult to persuade a worker to work and to the effort which, from the aspect of income need, he has least inducement to exert.

The second most frequent type of dispute resulting in open industrial conflict is that group of causes which I have described as union, inter-union and demarcation questions. These disputes, so far as they concern the type of labour to be employed, may in conditions of full employment give rise to less serious conflict than in the past if full employment is attained not merely as a passing phase but as a permanent feature of industrial life. The fear of unemployment is at the root of much of the opposition which exists to any change in established customs as to the type of labour to be employed. The assurance of adequate opportunities for alternative employment will eliminate much of the industrial unrest associated with changes of method essential in dynamic industrial conditions provided certain guarantees are given to the worker. First, there must be, as a matter of policy in industry both at the works and at higher levels, close consultation between management and workers as to such changes before they take place. Secondly, there must be arrangements which will operate not merely by the efflux of time but with a rapidity which has so far not been seen for dealing with displaced workers. The displaced worker, if his opposition to displacement is to be overcome, will expect some clearer knowledge than he has had in the past of where and when his skill will be employed and he will expect that knowledge prior to his displacement. In conditions of full employment this is a task of which the difficulties should not prove insuperable, and it is a field which will afford opportunities for the closest collaboration between employers, trade unions and the State in eliminating some of the time lags which, even in the stringency of war-time shortage of labour, have characterised the man-power situation.

The inter-union type of dispute is of rather a different nature and calls for serious attention by the workers and their organisations. In it the employer is often helpless and his intervention is certain to be resented by one or both of the disputants. Such disputes are from their nature peculiarly intractable, as workers regard them as vital to the organisational strength of the body they have chosen to represent them. The trade union movement has for long been alive to this problem and has endeavoured to promote amalgamation and other working arrangements between competing unions. Each year sees a decrease in the number of unions while the total membership continues to increase, but even at the end of 1943 two-thirds of the total number of unions (648 out of 972) accounted for only 2 % of the total membership of trade unions and each of these 648 separate unions had less than 1000 members. Many of these small unions are quite efficient in their sphere and many of them, being purely local, are not competitive. Indeed many of the inter-union disputes arise between large and powerful unions. The difficulties arising however from a multiplicity of small unions are very real and must be tackled with determination by the trade union movement. The trade union movement must find means of surmounting the legal obstacles and the vested interests which hinder amalgamation of unions if it is to remove one of the most serious defects in its structure. The trade union movement must improve its machinery for dealing with inter-union disputes and should offer employers the right to refer for decision to the Disputes Committee of the Trades Union Congress, or to a joint body of employers and workers, competing claims by unions for recognition within a works or an industry.

Hesitancy on the part of the Trades Union Congress—which has grown to its present influential position as a body which does not infringe the autonomy of its constituent unions—is understandable in face of the example of the divisions in the United States trade union movement which have resulted from attempts at greater central control. If the trade union movement however does not itself provide effective machinery accessible to the employer, the alternative seems to be the less desirable course which has been adopted in the United States of a government agency conducting elections in the works to determine which of competing unions should be recognised to represent the workers in that establishment. Legal compulsion to recognise trade unions is a poor substitute for the degree of voluntary acceptance which, after years of sometimes bitter strife, has been achieved in this country.

The non-unionist in almost any large factory is a cause of irritation to his fellow-workers and has become a source of disharmony which makes him unwelcome to most employers. The degree of action which should be taken to eliminate this cause of industrial friction is a matter of controversy. Agreements to employ only union men or to withhold certain wages advantages from non-unionists savour too much of dictation to be really popular in this country and would do the trade union movement more harm than good. Co-operation on the part of management and unions to demonstrate the advantages to industry of effective organisation can in the end achieve better results, especially if the trade union movement can assure to the worker impartial consideration by his union of causes of grievance against the union itself.

The third of the main groups of causes giving rise to industrial disputes is the class which I have described as disciplinary cases. Unemployment, or the fear of it, has in the past been the most powerful influence in maintenance of authority and discipline in industry. If it is agreed that authority and discipline are necessary to the conduct of industry, whether privately or publicly managed, and if dismissal for disciplinary reasons is to lose its terrors, other and better methods for the maintenance of authority and discipline will require to be sought. In full employment the necessity to dismiss a worker for disciplinary reasons may well be a greater hardship to the employer who cannot replace the dismissed worker than to the worker who can easily find alternative employment. The origin of most disciplinary troubles is the refusal by a worker to obey an order which he does not regard as reasonable and the equal reluctance of the manager to have his works stopped while a committee debates the reasonableness of the order. How can the two opposing attitudes be reconciled? There must be a recognition on the part of the workers that discipline is a necessity of industry and there must be a recognition on the part of the management that affirmation of the foreman or manager is not the sole test of the reasonableness of an order. Orders must be capable of being called in question at the proper time and place, but the proper time and place are not in the middle of the industrial process and on the workshop floor. There must be assurance to the management of obedience to its orders, and there must be assurance to the worker of subsequent joint investigation of his complaints leading to reversal for the future of unreasonable managerial decisions. The more serious type of disciplinary dispute would be peculiarly suitable for removal from the heated atmosphere of the works in which it has arisen so as to allow the persons involved to state their case before a committee of employers and workers from other works in the same industry who might in the course of time develop a habit of treating such matters judicially.

I have attempted to place before you in the course of this

lecture some of the main causes of industrial stoppages. I have expressed the view that most of them are likely to operate even more actively and to be even more difficult of solution in conditions of full employment. If I have ventured to suggest in broad outline improvements in the methods of industrial relations which might assist in preventing such disputes and in handling them if they do arise, the real purpose I had in mind was to state the problems rather than to solve them, to demonstrate the need for vigilance rather than complacency, to urge the importance of investigation of the methods of industrial relations, and to emphasise the essential part which the trade union and the employers' association will be called upon to play both in achieving and in maintaining full employment. The misery and wastefulness of unemployment are no less when the cause is a strike or lock-out which by our own direct efforts we could have prevented than when the cause lies in matters of international trade which only concerted international action can remedy.

The avoidance of stoppages arising from industrial disputes is however only the negative aspect of the problems of full employment. The positive side is largely the field of the technician and the scientist, but here also the worker in industrial relations has his part to play. The achievement of full employment itself and the benefits to be derived from it in the shape of a rising standard of real wages, shortening of working hours, and increased social security benefits can come only from increased productivity per hour of labour. Increased mechanisation and improvement of industrial methods are doubtless the most important factors but their full effectiveness depends on the willing co-operation of those engaged in industry to employ them to the best advantage. Only those with experience both of industrial relations and production problems know the very real influence of the works atmosphere on output. Without any deliberate policy of restriction of output, an atmosphere of hostility between management and men can play havoc with production. Works atmosphere depends both on personalities and on procedure. It can be poisoned by mere foolish lack of tact; it can be purified by human understanding. In all but the smallest undertakings personal contact between the higher management and the workers is not possible, and a recognised procedure of consultation becomes necessary for ensuring concerted effort towards maximum production. Joint committees for this purpose have existed for many years in individual establishments with varying degrees of success. They have been widely extended during the war under the title of Joint Production Consultative and Advisory Committees. Unfortunately in the establishments where the atmosphere is worst and their need is most pressing their hope of immediate success is least. It is better, however, that hard words should be spoken openly across the committee table where they can be answered with reason even if without immediate persuasion than whispered in the workshop or shouted from the soap box.

Joint consultation on production matters is also recognised and reasonably well-developed on a regional and national basis through the Regional Boards and National Production Advisory Council representing Government Departments and the central national bodies of employers and workers. The continuation of this form of joint consultation in peace time may prove of the utmost importance in organising production for the export trade, but it will still leave a gap in the sense that there are comparatively few industries where regular machinery exists for joint consultation at the national level on the peculiar production problems of that industry. Development of such machinery would provide completeness to the logical pattern of joint machinery for dealing locally and nationally in the individual industries and centrally for all industries with production problems such as already exists for dealing with labour problems.

More, however, is required than machinery. The success of the machinery depends not only on the willingness of employers to operate such machinery, to place their problems before it, to face criticism of their policy and methods and to answer it. Success depends not only on the co-operation of individual workers who sit on committees. It depends also and in the ultimate on the fundamental objectives of the trade union movement.

In propounding in 1927 a number of possible alternatives as to the conception of trade union aims, Sir Walter Citrine, the General Secretary of the Trades Union Congress, suggested as the one which was most likely to guide the representatives of the organised movement 'that the unions should actively participate in a concerted effort to raise industry to its highest efficiency by developing the most scientific methods of production, eliminating waste and harmful restrictions, removing causes of friction and avoidable conflict, and promoting the largest possible output so as to provide a rising standard of life and continuously improving conditions of employment'. That is one possible attitude, but there are others, and in particular there is the attitude of those who consider that to increase the efficiency of industry is merely to postpone the inevitable and desirable breakdown of the present system.

These two attitudes present a dilemma for the trade union and perhaps even more so for the trade unionist. There has, in the history of the trade union movement, been an oscillation between the emphasis placed on the one attitude and on the other, between the attitude of those who wished to see industry prosper in the meantime whatever their views as to the ultimate form of its control and the attitude of those who were so impressed by the need for radical change that they have been prepared to achieve it whatever the immediate cost. The dominating demand of organised labour, it is true, has throughout been for immediate improvement in the material conditions of the workers. Nevertheless, existence even in the background of the theory of the necessity of industrial action as distinct from political action, of non-co-operation in industry as an essential if the ultimate political aims of labour were to be achieved, has in some industries to a great extent and in all industries to some extent deprived industrial progress and efficiency of the spontaneity and enthusiasm they have achieved in the United States of America.

Such a confusion between industrial and political aims dates of course from the days when industrial action was necessary to bring political pressure to bear, when unions were fighting against outlawry, when the working man had the weapon of the strike but only in rare cases the vote. Its persistence into the days of universal suffrage was illogical but excused as necessary on the plea that the economic influence of certain classes by some mysterious means negatived the votes of the masses. Now that political events have demonstrated the contrary, we may hope that the workers will draw a clear distinction between industrial action and political action; that the trade union movement as a whole and without reservation will devote its energies in the industrial sphere to increasing the efficiency of industry and improving the standard of life of those engaged in it; that it will use political means, and political means

(23)

only, for bringing about any changes in the structure of industry which it regards as necessary for the ultimate well-being of the community. In very different circumstances from those of the present day, a national conference of trade unions met in London exactly a hundred years ago and had before it a report from the London Committee of Trade Delegates in which it was adjured 'to keep trade matters and politics as distinct as circumstances will justify'. Political events which could not be visualised then may provide an opportunity to-day of acting on such advice.

The problems of industrial relations in conditions of full employment are real but they should not be exaggerated. They can be handled successfully and the difficulties overcome if those responsible for industrial negotiations approach them with a real desire to make the system work, if they can devise means for dealing effectively with unauthorised and unofficial action within their own ranks, and if the field of controversy in industrial relations can be narrowed by eliminating unnecessary anomalies between different occupations and industries. But the task which is set the industrial negotiator must itself be a reasonable one. The industrial relations in any industry are not the sphere in which major matters of national policy such as the ownership and control of industry and national financial policy should be fought out and decided. Such matters are irrelevant to industrial relations, not because they lack importance, but because their paramount importance demands their discussion and decision in a wider sphere.

The responsibility which the community entrusts to those who handle industrial relations has been great in the past and may well prove greater in the future even if irrelevancies are dismissed. The community has a right to demand that the responsibility should be discharged in no narrow manner but in the interests of the community as a whole, and that the community should have the means of satisfying itself of the manner of the discharge.

Lastly, therefore, I would make a plea for more publicity in the affairs and methods of employers' associations and trade unions. Mystery was appropriate to the days when combination was a crime and associations of workmen were secret societies hunted by the law. Now that trade unions and employers' associations have become chosen instruments of public policy, industrial agreements regulating conditions of employment in any industry should be available in intelligible form to all other industries and to the public, so that one industry may know the conditions of another and so that the public may judge of the merits of industrial agreements concluded and industrial disputes which emerge. An official Report on Collective Agreements was published in 1910. The first volume of a new Report was published by the Ministry of Labour in 1934, but the Report was never completed. A new Report is urgently needed, but it is not sufficient to prepare a work of this nature at intervals of a quarter of a century or even of a decade. The study and the practice of industrial relations require not only the production at reasonable intervals of a complete Report but the prompt publication and annotation in a supplement to the Ministry of Labour Gazette of the texts of all important industrial agreements and awards as they are made.

There is no finality in industrial relations. There is need for continual study; above all there is need for regular and accurate information. He who teaches industrial relations must continue to learn and in learning he may learn the better to teach. I began this lecture by quoting the words used in an Inaugural Lecture before this University by a famous Englishman. It may be permitted to me to conclude by quoting the words used by a notable Scotsman, A. J. Scott, who in his Inaugural Address nearly a hundred years ago as the first Principal of Owens College, Manchester, said:

'He who learns from one occupied in learning, drinks of a running stream. He who learns from one who has learned all he is to teach, drinks the green mantle of the stagnant pool.'